ARTICLE MARKETING SIMPLIFIED

ANTHONY EKANEM

ISBN 979-888521149-9

Contents

Preface

Of all the ways to make money online, in my opinion, article marketing is the easiest and best way for anybody to make their first dollar. The best part is that without spending any more than the cost of a domain name, you can create a passive income that can bring you money from an article that you wrote years ago. So, ask yourself: "Is spending a few minutes writing a 250-word article worth the time if it will bring you money years later?" I suppose "yes" would be the answer.

I'm sure you've heard a ton of different opinions on how you should do article marketing and how you should provide the best information possible, write informative articles and give your reader value and so on. Well, what you're about to read is probably going to go against a lot of what you have read, and the article "gurus" are not going to like it but doing it this way has made me a lot of money, so I don't care if they agree with me or not! I'm going to do it the way it makes money and a way that continues to bring me money day in and day out.

If you are willing to put in the time to follow this method, you will make moneyand a good amount of it. What you need to remember is that there is no superhighway to making money on the Internet. You must stay consistent and motivated even when you get frustrated and feel like things are not going your way. It is those who continue to work and promote their business that will in the end be successful.

So, no more pep talks. Let's get right into it.

CHAPTER ONE

What Is Article Marketing?

Article Marketing is essentially writing and distributing short articles to a variety of outlets, including article repositories, which are also called article directories and article banks, forums, and newsletter publishers. Article marketing is one of the most effective types of marketing that one can do – it is also one of the least expensive ways to market a business. It can even be free, costing you nothing more than your time.

There are many benefits to article marketing. Because articles become viral, your message travels far and wide, increasing traffic to your website and increasing newsletter signups. Article marketing is also used to make sales and to build credibility. Anyone who wants to establish themselves as an expert in their niche should take advantage of all that article marketing has to offer.

Here is how it works. Let's say that you are in the weight loss niche, and you sell various weight loss products, whether they are your products or products of which you are an affiliate. You write a weight loss article, preferably one that is closely related to one of your products – but you don't want to necessarily advertise the product in the article.

Instead, you want to address a problem that the product can help to solve in your article – without mentioning the product. For instance, if you sell a cellulite cream, you can write an article about what cellulite is, what causes it, and the various methods used to get rid of it. The article should be no more than 750 words and have a compelling title.

At the bottom of your article, you include an author's resource box. This is a block of text, made up of one paragraph that is anywhere from five to seven lines long. In this paragraph, you might say something like this:

John Doe is a weight loss expert who has helped hundreds of people get and keep weight off. You can find more valuable weight loss information and help at his website, John Doe's Weight Loss Secrets, located athttp://www.johndoe.com. You can find specific information for getting rid of cellulite at http://www.johndoe.com/cellulite.html.

Once you have written your article, ensure that you have made all the points that you wanted to make, and checked the article for spelling and grammar mistakes, you are ready to distribute it.

Distributing an article can be a very time-consuming task. Many people outsource this work and pay a fee for someone else to do the distribution work. Others do it themselves using software that automates the process. You should note, however, that many article repositories do not allow or approve articles that are auto-submitted – and they can tell when this is done. Manual submissions – whether done by you or someone else – is always the best.

The article is distributed to the article repositories first. There are hundreds of these in existence, and some are better than others. For these repositories, you will need your article, the title, possibly a subtitle, your author's resource box, your website URL, your email address, a short description of your article, and a list of keywords, separated by commas, for your article.

Essentially, you visit each article repository, either sign up for a new account or log in and copy and paste all the information into a form that is provided for article submissions. Most article repositories have a manual approval process, so it may take a week or more before your article appears on their website.

Once you have submitted it to the article repositories, you will want to distribute your article to ezine publishers that cover topics within your niche. You can build your database of these publishers. You find them by visiting the ezine directories.

Look first for ezines in your niche, and then check each ezine to see if they accept articles. Load those article submission email addresses into your autoresponder, and each time you write a new article, send it to these publishers, asking them to publish the article.

Next, you visit forums that are of interest to your target market. If your niche is weight loss, you visit weight loss forums and look to see if they have a place for articles. If so, submit your article there. If not, post the article on your website, and then become an active member in the forum. If your article is about cellulite, look for posts concerning cellulite.

It is perfectly acceptable to make a post and say that you have an article about this on your website and leave the link directly to the article. Just make sure that your post is relevant and on topic, and that your article provides useful information that is also relevant.

All of this is essentially what article marketing is, and how it is done, however, there is a great deal more to learn and know about article marketing to become successful at it.

CHAPTER TWO

The History of Article Marketing

Article marketing has been around almost if the Internet has been around – even though it wasn't meant for actual marketing purposes. Many years ago, back in the '90s, people shared information. This was termed 'the spirit of the Internet' way back then, and that spirit still exists today, even though it isn't as obvious.

The Internet was designed for the free and fast exchange of information. People wrote articles on a variety of topics, to share information and educate others. At first, there weren't any article repositories. Newsletters, also called ezines, came into play long before article banks did. So, when you wanted to share an article with the Internet community, you posted the article on your website, in a Usenet newsgroup, or your ezine. Eventually, people started allowing other ezine publishers to use their articles as well – and the author's resource box was born.

Because articles had such an impact in each niche (niche being another word that wasn't used at that time), intelligent marketers saw the potential for writing and distributing articles – freely –to promote their businesses. They started writing and distributing articles regularly –

and article marketing was born – even though it wasn't necessarily called that then. It was simply called 'writing and distributing articles.'

Those articles were formatted much the way that articles are formatted today, except HTML tags were not used. The articles were all text, just as many are today. However, while links in the article are hyperlinked today, they were not hyperlinked back then, in most cases. In case you don't know, when a link is hyperlinked, the reader can simply click on the link to visit the webpage. When it is not hyperlinked, the reader must copy and paste the URL into their web browser, or type it in.

Over time, people learned that some measure of copywriting skills were needed for article marketing, to write outstanding, attention-getting headlines, and to create an effective author's resource box. Even though writing and distributing articles was turning out to be an effective and cost-effective way to market a business, the articles that were written and distributed were of very high quality. The spirit of the Internet was still very visible and in full swing.

The articles were written more to share information, and less to market a business – yet business owners who were doing this were thriving because of it. At that time, we were not inundated with information. There was no information overload, and nobody would dare write a sales letter and try to disguise it as an article. That's what solo ads in ezines were for – sales letters. Articles, on the other hand, were helpful to those reading them.

Over the years, newbie marketers came on the scene and saw article marketing as an opportunity – but did not fully understand or pay attention to the spirit of the Internet – the free exchange of information on a global scale. This is when sales articles started appearing. Those newbie marketers soon learned that they wouldn't get anywhere with this type of article marketing. Some gave up; others changed their ways and started doing it right.

It's hard to say when the first article repository was born. Before that, however, articles were just sent to ezine publishers directly and posted to newsgroups. However, article announcement email lists came into play – where people could more easily get their articles into the hands of ezine publishers and web publishers.

Those announcement lists were very good, for a very long time, but they eventually played out, just as FFA Link sites played out. People were participating only to distribute their articles but were not reading or using other people's articles. However, those announcement lists did have a nice long run, and many people still use them today just for the small results that they get.

For the most part, however, article marketing is done today just as it was in the beginning, with very few differences. Article marketing is one of the few types of Internet Marketing methods that have remained the same, without losing any of its effectiveness.

Furthermore, article marketing is also one of the few marketing methods that have been able to stand the test of time, regardless of changes that have been made to search engines, the way people buy on the Internet or even laws that have changed – such as the spamming laws. None of the changes that have been made has had any impact, and there is no impact expected in the future as well.

CHAPTER THREE

Article Marketing Today

Again, article marketing hasn't changed much. What worked in article marketing in the past, still works today – except that the announcement lists aren't as effective for getting your article out. There have been many attempts, however, to change article marketing, in terms of writing and distributing. Some of those new methods are successful, while others are not.

For instance, in recent years, automated submission software has come into the picture. This worked for a while, greatly speeding up the submission process, but most of the top article directories now block such software and reject articles that are auto-submitted. The owners of those directories understand that such software could eventually make article marketing a thing of the past.

There has been software created to help one write articles. While this is useful software, what people don't realize is that it still takes some degree of writing skill to produce a quality article. This software is not 100% effective. What most people do now if they don't have the writing skills that article marketing demands, is to hire ghostwriters to write their articles for them.

Unfortunately, not everyone who calls themselves a writer is. Some of the so-called writers out there have worse writing skills than the person seeking help! Many don't even speak English.

Hiring a ghostwriter is perfectly acceptable. First, nobody knows that you did not write the article yourself. If you choose a good ghostwriter, you will have quality articles that do what they were meant to do. You will also find that the cost of a ghostwriter is quite reasonable.

Most people hire a ghostwriter and then have the writer write a couple of articles to see how well they do, and then stick with the ghostwriter long term when they see that the ghostwriter can accomplish the task effectively.

In the past year or so, numerous new article repositories have popped up around the Internet. This is due to the release (and sale) of article directory scripts. You see, owning and operating an article directory can make you money. People come to your site to submit their articles to your directory. While they are there, they may view AdSense ads or other ads that are on your site. Since they register for your site to be able to submit articles, you are also now able to send them emails as well.

If the article directory site is promoted properly by the owner, he or she makes additional money by placing AdSense or other ads on all the article pages. This does not hurt the author of the articles in any way. The key here is that the site must be promoted by the owner for it to gain popularity. While submitting to these newcomers may not be very beneficial to the author of the article now, it will be beneficial in the future – once the site has aged and become popular.

There are numerous courses available now that teach the art of article marketing today as well. In the past, it was something that you had to figure out on your own. Today, there is help. There is free information, as well as paid information. If you need to learn, the free information will give you the help you need to get started in the right direction, but the paid information is what you will need to succeed and get the most benefits out of article marketing.

As in the past, there are still newcomers to Internet Marketing who don't understand the spirit of the Internet. You will still see articles, from time to time, that are nothing more than sales letters. Thankfully, however, the people who run the most authoritative article repositories don't allow such articles to make it into their database. Articles are still usually manually viewed and approved before they are published on these sites.

Article theft, where someone takes your article and removes your name, trying to pass it off as their work, has become a small problem. But for the most part, this problem doesn't have a large impact on the Internet community. Usually, when the offender is called out and informed of the legal ramifications, the article is removed.

No matter what new methods come into play, one thing will always remain the same. To be successful at article marketing, you must turn out quality articles that serve to help, inform, or educate people. This is the only way that you will be rewarded for your efforts because the spirit of the Internet does exist – and it's here to stay.

CHAPTER FOUR

The Future of Article Marketing

As stated, article marketing is here to stay. It is a stable method of marketing that simply is not going away, no matter what changes may occur in the online world. Because article marketing is here to stay, it is something that will benefit you today and in the future.

The article marketing that you do today will still be benefiting you ten years from now. Article marketing is viral, and it's a virus that can't be killed. You see, when you take the time to write and distribute an article, other people, such as web publishers, bloggers, and ezine publishers, will use your articles on their websites, in their newsletters, and on their blogs.

People who read their websites, blogs, and newsletters will also use your articles on *their* websites, newsletters, and blogs, as will *their* visitors. The process just keeps going and going, for as long as the information in your article remains relevant to the current trends or the information does not change. Believe it or not, methods may change, information, however, rarely changes.

While many of the new article repositories may not be around in the future, some have been around since the first article repository made its appearance. The longevity of an article repository depends on how well it is promoted, and how long the person who owns the article repository decides to stay in business.

When you submit to one of these article banks, your article will remain on that site for as long as that site exists. But even if the site doesn't exist ten years from now, you still benefit from the article that you submitted there when it did exist – because other people visit, read your article, and use it elsewhere.

Even with the abundance of information on the Internet, and the information overload that exists, people still need and use articles – and people still read them every day. While personal computers are in millions of homes, each day, more and more people purchase their first computers and surf the Internet – looking for information about their interests, problems that they are experiencing, or things that they want to learn. They find the information that they are seeking on websites, blogs, and newsletters – all of which are publishing articles. The key to article marketing is to find your niche and hone it. Often, people don't pay attention when submitting articles.

For instance, an article that fits into the weight loss niche has no place in an article repository that was set up solely for web design articles. While many repositories accept articles on a large variety of topics – some only accept articles that relate to a specific topic. Usually, the people who are submitting articles to the wrong directories are also the people who are writing sales letters, calling them articles, and then using automated software to distribute those sales letters.

As in the past, marketing methods will come and go. It's getting harder to send emails. It's getting harder to get listed in the search engines. It's getting harder to use Pay-Per-Click search engines. The rules are constantly changing – and they change so incredibly fast that most marketers can't keep up with all of it.

But article marketing will remain. The changing rules that affect other methods of marketing will not affect article marketing, for the most part. There may come a time when it is no longer safe to email ezine publishers – but even if that happens, another method for getting your articles in the right hands will come along to replace that method.

Some people wonder about the influx of article writers and what part that will play in the effectiveness of article marketing. For the most part, it won't have any impact at all. You see, because we now have the Internet, and we live in a global society, we still crave information – and even with information overload, we still can't seem to get enough!

We are a species that is capable of thought – intelligent thought – and therefore, we understand the importance of hearing or reading varying viewpoints on different topics. We thrive on it. Few people read articles within a specific niche that are written by just one author – we want to hear what other experts say as well – just as we get second opinions for medical diagnosis, and often third and fourth opinions as well. This is why the influx of people who are using article marketing for their businesses won't hurt the effectiveness of article marketing. As long as there are people in the world, information will be needed...even if it is information that has been published time and time again.

Again, article marketing may change – but it will only change in ways that make it better. There may be gimmicks that come and go that are designed to make article marketing better, faster, or easier – but any way you look at it, what works today will work tomorrow where article marketing is concerned, and for all intents and purposes, the results that people see from article marketing will also remain just as they are today – and just as they were in the past.

CHAPTER FIVE

Article Marketing for Your Business

If you are not already using article marketing for your business, you are missing out on sales and signups that could be garnered from this time-tested method of marketing a business online. Anyone who isn't already marketing their business with articles should get started on it right away.

Remember, your article marketing efforts of today will continue to pay off for years to come. You can't say that about any other type of marketing that exists. For the future of your business, this is an area of marketing that you need to learn – and you need to learn every aspect of it as soon as possible.

You may shy away from article marketing because you can't write well, or because you don't think that article marketing is right for your niche. These are valid reasons – but they are wrong. Even if you can't write well, you can pay someone who does. Having articles written is surprisingly cheap. You can have one article written every week for less than ten dollars.

You can also take one of the many free writing courses online to learn how to write articles. Once you get the hang of writing articles, you will find that you can write a short article in less than half an hour. If you are slow at typing, or your article will require more research, you can knock one out in about an hour.

As for article marketing not being right for your niche – wrong again. Article marketing works for all niches. Have you been to a search engine lately? No matter what you think of typing in, you will find web pages on that topic. Where there are web pages, there are readers, and where there are readers, there is a need for articles.

Go ahead – try it. Visit your favourite search engine and try to think up something off the wall and type it in. You will find web pages that have content on them! Web content comes from articles – whether they are articles that were written specifically for that website, or articles that were found in the article banks.

You may not think you have time for article distribution. You can pay someone to do this, but the fact of the matter is that even if you just submitted your article to ten article banks each week, you will still benefit. You will benefit even more if you submit to more article banks, publishers, and forums – but just ten will work as well. Doing nothing at all, however, won't get you anywhere at all. It takes less than one hour to submit to ten article directories.

So, if you have an article written for you, and you submit it to ten directories, you are looking at half an hour of work a week. If you write the article yourself and submit it, you are looking at about two hours per week. If you outsource all of it – writing and distribution, you are looking at ten minutes a week or less – and this includes sending an email to your writer and paying them once the work is done, once you find a ghostwriter that you want to work with continuingly.

You have everything to gain from article marketing, and nothing to lose – if you are doing your article marketing in the right way. Even if you did it in the wrong way, the most you stand to lose is your time. Frankly, article marketing is hard to fail at.

The process is incredibly simple: write an informative article, include a resource box that has a call to action, distribute the article, and reap the benefits for years to come. That's all there is to it – and this is a marketing method that is available to everyone – even if they are new to Internet Business. You don't have to be a guru to write articles. You become a guru by writing articles.

You don't even have to own a business to start writing articles and profiting from them. Affiliate marketing, where you promote other people's products and services for a percentage of each sale, can easily be done through article marketing – and this is where many gurus got their start.

If you aren't article marketing, you are leaving money on the table. It is as simple as that – and you can start article marketing today. Right now. If you can write, write. If you can't, hire a ghostwriter, pay eight to ten bucks for the article, and start distributing it. All of that can be done now – today.

Don't let another day go by that you are not benefiting from the uncontested and unrivalled effectiveness of article marketing! The future of your business, as well as your financial future, could depend on it.

Automating Your Article Marketing?

The only problem that many internet marketers have is the time you have to put in for article marketing to be effective. Most experienced internet marketers know that the more time you put in, the more you get out, but newer marketers, especially, want to find shortcuts.

So, can you find shortcuts for article marketing? Is it possible to shortcut your way through keyword and article research? Is it possible to automate the tedious work of writing article after article from scratch and then submitting them to hundreds of article directories manually?

The answer is – YES! As many guru article marketers know, there is software available to make keyword research, article writing and submission easier by automating it. If you have the right software tools and loads of Niche PLR articles, you can jump-start your article writing by automating a lot of tedious tasks, like creating hundreds of unique articles and submitting them to hundreds of top article directories with the press of a button.

CHAPTER SIX

Picking a Niche Made Easy

I'm not going to go deep into this as there are tons of easy ways to find a niche. But I will give you, in my opinion, the easiest way to find one. Here's how I pick a niche. I look at ONE thing when I'm going to pick a niche. Is there a problem that someone needs a solution to? Now, I'm not going to say this is the only way to pick a niche, but I have found it to be most profitable.

Think about that for a minute. If a person has a problem and they are looking for a solution, they will almost definitely buy something that will give them that solution if you can convince them, you can provide it to them. In my opinion, a problem is much more profitable than a hobby or a curiosity. When people have problems or issues, they want answers and a solution, and they want it fast! And if you can convince them, you have the solution, guess what? You're going to get that sale!

So, when picking a niche, put yourself in the position of the buyer. If you had a certain problem such as a "yeast infection" and you have been struggling with curing it for a while, would you pay for a solution? Right, you would! Now don't confuse "wants" with "problems". Weight loss for instance is not necessarily a "problem". It can be a problem but wanting to lose weight is just that, "wanting to".

Now, if a person has high blood pressure, that's a problem. That's something that a person would want to fix and fix fast! Having a yeast infection is a problem and is also a thing that a person would want to be solved. Don't get me wrong, there is a lot of money in the "weight loss" niche just as there is a lot of money in the "make money online" niche, but they are tough to get a consistent piece of the pie. You will do much better and much faster if you get into things that will give people solutions to problems quickly.

This can go deep into this thought process as well into other niches. If a person is big into video games but can't seem to get past a certain level, they have a problem. They will be willing to pay if you can provide them with a way to get past that level. Panic attacks are a problem, skin tabs are a problem, heartburn is a problem, feeling like your spouse is cheating is a problem, playing basketball and not being able to jump very high is a problem, having a virus on your computer and tinnitus (constant ringing in the ear) are problems.

Find the niches that people are desperate for a solution to a problem, and you'll find the money you are looking for! Once you've thought of a problem or looked around Yahoo! Answers to see what people are having problems with, it's time to go to ClickBank.com and see if there is a product that will solve this problem. Chances are you will find more than one. Look at the products offered and see which one converts the best. You can tell this by the gravity of the product. Once you've selected the "problem" you're going to fix, and the product you're going to promote to solve it, it's time to get ready to start getting set up.

Getting Set Up

The next thing you are going to do is called *Keyword Research*. There are tons of different ways to do this, but here's how I do it. I use Micro Niche Finder as it saves me a lot of time. However, if you don't want to spend the money on a keyword tool, then you can use the Google AdWords Tool or the free version of Word Tracker. What you are looking for is keywords that people will be typing into Google to find solutions to their problems. If you're using Micro Niche Finder, all you must do is type in a keyword phrase and it will bring you back all the keyword phrases that go along with the one you typed in. It will also show you the daily search volumes as well as the competition for each phrase.

If you are looking for keywords the manual way, type in the keyword phrase you are looking at using into either one of the free tools listed above. They will both bring you back phrases that go along with the one you typed in. Make sure you check the competition of these phrases by putting "quotes" around the keywords. Also, if you are going to use the Google AdWords Tool, make sure you set the tool on "exact" instead of the default "broad" it's set to. If you don't, you will get keywords that will claim to get thousands of searches a month when they don't get any.

The easiest way to find some good keywords is to go over to Ezine Articles and look up other articles that are written about the same subject you are targeting. Once on that article, hit the "view" button on the top of your browser. The drop-down box will open, and you will click on the "source" tab. You will then see the code for the article. You will then see a lot of codes. Here is what you're looking for: *<meta name="keywords" content="catch a cheater">*. I pulled this from an article about catching a cheating spouse. This article was targeted around the keyword "catch a cheater". Now you can find some great keywords this way. The grunt work has already been done for you when you use this method, all you must do is put in one of the keyword tools to see the daily searches and check the competition. I'm all about making things easy, and this is one of the easiest ways to find some golden keywords. Let other people spend long hours searching for that golden keyword. You can just scoop it up in seconds using this method.

I would start by getting about 10 keywords that you want to go after. If you can find a keyword that has 60 or more searches a day with less than 10,000 competitions, you have found yourself a gold mine. With article marketing, I try not to go after anything that has less than 30 searches a day or 900 a month. As far as competition, I won't go after anything with more than about 35,000 competitions. That's not saying that you can't go after a keyword phrase with more competition than that because you can. But for the fastest success, I would keep it under 20,000. The lower the competition the better chance you have of getting your article ranking on the front page of Google, which is where we are going to end up with this.

Try and find "buying" keywords that start with things like "where to buy" or "get something". The more targeted you are with keywords that are "buying" keywords, the better your results. If you want to get good at keyword research, John Orna has in my opinion, the best keyword research book available. He's got a little trick at the end that deals with Google analytics and a quick AdWords campaign that will give you an advantage. The book is called *Digging for Gold.*

Finally, once you have done keyword research for your product, go to EzineArticles and create an account to submit your articles.

Now you are all set up and it's time to start making money!

CHAPTER SEVEN

Writing Your Articles Step by Step

Here's where you will get a ton of different opinions on how your article will be most effective. You will hear many say you must have great information in your article if you want to "catch" your customers and get them to click on the link. I completely disagree. I don't think you have to give them any real information if you want to be successful and honestly, I believe the less information you give them the better off you are. I know that sounds crazy but trust me it works.

I also don't believe that you must write your articles at a pace of 500 words per article. I think that is way too much! I don't write articles that are over 300 words ever! If I do, it was an accident. The only piece of copy that needs to be about 500 words is the landing page content or the article you are going to ultimately link to.

There are three reasons for this. The first is that I want the person reading my article to be able to see my link in my resource box no matter where they are in the article. This way even if they don't finish it, they can still see there is a place to visit behind the link. Second, I think 500 words is just too long to keep a person's attention long enough to finish the article without getting bored and leaving before clicking your link.

Now, here's where people will say "if you write a good enough article", but why waste my time when I can get better results in half the words and 1/3 of the time. Time is money after all, and you'll get to the point where you can write about any topic you want and not have hardly any research at all!

Third, the last thing you want to do is give out too much information and if you are writing 500 words, there's a good bet that you've given them too much information, or at least enough to make them think they can try to fix their problem on their own. Even though they probably won't be able to, it won't stop them from trying. And once they figure out, they can't fix it themselves, the chances of their getting back to your article and clicking on your link are less of a percentage than I care to combat against.

So, the first thing is to keep your articles short! 250-300 words max is what you should shoot for. Again, some will disagree with this, but most of them either run article directories themselves and a short article won't help their directories page rank, or they are trying to brand themselves as an expert in their field. We are trying to do neither with this method. I'll go into this more later.

Now that we have already decided that we are going to keep our articles short, we can get into the actual writing of the article. There are three aspects to this. They are:

1. The Title
2. The body
3. The resource box

We'll tackle them in order, and I'll show you how to get the most out of each one.

Writing the Title

To me, the title is the most important part of the article. Now that might sound crazy, but if you have a boring title then nobody is going to open your article! If nobody opens your article, then there's no way you're going to make any money. So, the title is the most important part of your article – at least at first. So, when writing a title, you must get creative. There is nothing worse than a boring title. Let's take dog training for instance. First off, make sure you put your keyword phrase at the beginning of the title.

Having your keyword at the beginning of your title is a must! You can put it at the end, but for some reason, Google seems to give you better rankings if it's in the front. The first thing you want to do is make your title long! The reason for this is that it will stand out more than a short one. If you've got a list of 15 articles, the ones with the longer titles will stand out more and not just blend in as the short ones will. Don't overlook this tip! Long titles will always get more attention than short ones. Plus, you can get more creative with longer titles than short titles.

So, let's use "potty training my dog" as the keyword phrase we are going to use. There are two titles below, now read them and ask yourself which one you would open if you were someone searching for a solution to your dog taking a crap on the floor.

"Potty Training My Dog – Nobody likes an untrained dog"

Or

"Potty Training My Dog – Steps That Will Help You from Murdering Your Pet from Pissing on Your Couch"

Now, if you saw those two titles, which one would YOU open? Here's another example with the keyword "catch a cheater":

"Catch a Cheater – It Doesn't Feel Good to Think Your Spouse Is Cheating"

Or

"Catch a Cheater – Here's The Fastest Method to Catch a Filthy Cheater!"

Again, which one would you open? So, when you are creating your title, don't be scared to get a little creative with them. Here's another example of a good title: Get Your Ex Back with These Steps – Is Tying Them up Included? The more creative and "shocking" your titles are the more they will get opened. The more normal looks like everybody else's title yours is the fewer views you'll get. To sum up titles, make sure you put your keyword at the front of the article and get creative with it. Now we can get into writing the article.

Writing the Article Body

Now here's really where my method and others are going to vary. Most "article marketing gurus" will tell you that you must write 500-word articles and make them super informative to have any type of success. However, the way I do it goes completely against everything they say, and it works well! Do you think they all "follow" what they preach? Not hardly. Ready for the "secret"? play on people's emotions and don't give them any real information! That's all you must do. The truth is the less information you give them the better off your click-through rate is going to be. Why? Well, they went looking for information to solve a problem, they get to your article, and you play on their emotions, but you don't give them any information that will solve it. What you do give them is a place where they can find some information, and that is your link in the resource box. From there you let the products sales page do its job because that's what it's supposed to do!

Now you may think that's a little harsh, but you won't when you see money coming in! What do you think commercials on television do? If you analyze them, they are playing on people's emotions. You see a person on TV that has a bad acne problem, and they have this depressed look on their face. What they are doing is trying to show a person in a similar situation as someone who has acne and the depression and embarrassment that goes along with it. Then what happens next? You guessed it! The next frame shows this same person with a big smile on their face and exuding confidence. Why? Because their acne is gone. Then of course they show you the product and you think "hey, if it worked for them, maybe it will work for me." Now you don't know for sure if it will work, but if having acne is a big problem for you, you're going to be willing to take a chance that it will work!

But notice that they don't give you any "real" information as to how it's going to work, or they don't give you anything you can try on your own. If you want to get results, you're going to have to take your chances that that product is going to work. That's called good marketing and it's no different from what you're going to do with your articles.

And that's why we pick niches that have to do with solving people's problems. Let's take the "yeast infection" niche for instance. Now everybody knows what a yeast infection is. We also know that there is not a woman in the world that wants anyone to know that they are dealing with one. So were going to play on these facts:

1. They are embarrassing

2. Over the counter medications treat only the infections

3. They can cause vaginal odour

4. They can continue to come back if not treated properly.

You noticed in there that you won't find anything that gives you any advice on how to cure it. That's where your resource box comes in, but it is going to drill into a person dealing with one, the reasons they want it fixed. So below is an example of an article about yeast infections:

Example: Dealing with Vaginal Odour

Dealing With Vaginal Odor - Not only is it embarrassing but it is also upsetting for a Woman.

"Dealing with vaginal odour is a very embarrassing thing for a woman to deal with. Not only is it upsetting because you have an odour coming from the most private part of your body, but it is all so embarrassing that your spouse may notice it. Just think how it can ruin a person's sexual confidence! It can also be very embarrassing having to go to the Doctor to get some type of remedy. About 99% of the time, the reason a woman has a vaginal odour is due to an infection. Keep reading to find out what you can do to get rid of vaginal odour.

Most people will run to the store and purchase an over-the-counter medication when dealing with vaginal odour. The unfortunate thing is most people do not know that these medications do anything but treat the symptoms of an infection. Even doctors prescribed medications do nothing more than take care of the symptoms of a yeast infection. Some of the symptoms you may have are natural odour, itching, burning, vaginal discharge and swelling. To get rid of vaginal odour, you must treat the actual infection and not just the symptoms.

Many times, the actual infection is inside the intestines. Because doctor prescribed medications and over-the-counter remedies treat only the symptoms, the infection eventually comes back and just make a person more upset. Because of this, thousands of women are switching to certain home remedies when dealing with vaginal odour and yeast infections.

These remedies treat the actual infection itself not only the symptoms. The results that have been reported have been extremely positive. Not only have people been getting great results, but they are also able to do it from the comfort of their home saving them the embarrassment of letting someone else know they have a foul vaginal odour."

So, here's what we've done. We've reminded them it's embarrassing, we've let them know that buying over the counter medications and doctor prescriptions isn't going to help long term and that a lot of people are moving over to certain remedies for solutions.

We gave them no information about how they can try themselves to cure the yeast infection, but we did tell them there are "certain remedies" that have had extremely positive results that they can do from home. We've just planted in their mind that all the "normal" ways they would use to treat it are not going to give them a permanent cure so even if they haven't tried those yet, chances are they are not going to.

Put yourself in the shoes of the person who just read this. If you had this problem, would you click the link to at least look at the "certain remedies" that are being talked about? Yea, I think you would too. Now it's time for your resource box to finish the job. Here's the resource box I would use to end the article and let them know there is a solution to their problem on the other end of the link.

Example resource box:

If you are suffering from a yeast infection, here is my #1 recommended remedy for dealing with vaginal odour. This remedy gives you proven advice and guarantees that it will give you the best vaginal odour solution possible by clicking *here.* Now since our keyword is "dealing with

vaginal odour" you would hyperlink "dealing with vaginal odour" to the product sales page as well as a hyperlink "click here". We'll get more into resource boxes here in a second. Now that article is under 300 words, so no matter where the person is on that article, they can see those links in the resource box.

So, we have a good article here. It's short so they can see the links, it doesn't give them any information on how to solve their problem, it reminds them of the problems their condition is causing, and we give them a place where they can find a solution to the problem – your affiliate link! Now that we know how to write an article, let's get to the resource box.

Creating the Resource Box

The resource box in my opinion is no more important than the article body itself. If your article sucks, then it doesn't matter what your resource box says because no one is going to get down there to click it. They will leave long before. But since I've shown you how to write a good article that will make people get to the resource box, you want to have a good one when they get there. The first thing I want to get out of the way is that you should always have your keyword hyperlinked in your resource box. This helps you get ranked for that keyword and is a must! Always hyperlink your keyword in your resource box.

Once they have finished reading your article where you haven't given them a solution, they should be drooling to find one. You must make your resource box "reel them in" to your link. I like to use a resource box that again reminds them of the problem they have and then gives them the #1 recommended solution for it. Here's another example of a good resource box, but this time we'll use the heartburn niche.

"If you've had enough of dealing with the constant pain of heartburn no matter how you have tried to cure it, here is my #1 recommended solution to getting rid of heartburn. Stop the constant pain caused by this condition and find a solution by clicking here."

You would hyperlink "getting rid of heartburn" and "Clicking Here".

One thing I wanted to mention and here's another time a lot of Article Marketers and I are going to disagree, but I like using words like "click here" or "go here now". People say they don't work and that it just makes it look like it's nothing more than you are trying to sell something. The truth is that it works! Read that again, it works!

Another thing I don't like to see is when people use resource boxes that say stuff like: *"Joe Blow is a professional so and so that has been in the business since 1492. He has dealt with this for 400 years and knows all about this, that and the other. To see what he recommends, go to ww.blahblahblah.com"*

Those don't work most of the time and to be honest, nobody cares who Joe Blow is. People want solutions to their problems and don't care who it is that is going to give it to them. If you write a good article like I showed you, and follow it with a good resource box, they won't care who you are. They just want the answer to their problem!

This is also why I don't recommend filling out the Ezine Author Bio for any of the pen names you use. It just gives people another reason to click off your article and read something that can take their mind off what they just read. In the bio box, if I'm writing an article about yeast infections, I'll just put something like "Yeast infections are embarrassing, you don't have to deal with them any longer".

I don't fill out who the "author" is or their history. This may be necessary for things like weight loss or IM but not for problem-solving. I've tested this so I'm not just pulling it out of nowhere. During the test, the one without a bio got 11 more sales than the one that did. And I ran the test for a month.

Now, EzineArticles only allows you to redirect from a top-level domain name, so the links in your resource box will either be a redirect from a domain name you bought or a link to a landing page. You will either buy a domain name and redirect it to your affiliate link or build a landing page.

Again, a lot of people tell you that you need to have a presale page because it converts better. Sometimes yes and sometimes no, it just depends. I look at it this way, they're going to get to the affiliate's sales page at some point, so why not send them straight there and make sure it converts. If you write the article well and have them salivating for an answer, who needs a "presale" page. You just presold them.

I'll tell you this much if I get an article ranking on the top page of Google for a keyword, even if it was going to a landing page, I'm switching it to go straight to the affiliate's sales page. Of course, here again, is where many others will disagree with this, but I don't care! I'm going to do what puts money in my pocket and not what I'm "supposed" to do because everyone else does.

You can also send the traffic to squeeze pages and build yourself a list that you can keep pitching them a product or products over time. I would say building a list is the smartest way to build a long-term business. To a lot of people starting, this may not seem like the best idea, but I've come to find that it may be the smartest way for long term income.

That's it for writing the article. Now we get into all the things we can do with them to make money and get them ranking on the front page of Google!

What to Do with Your Articles

The writing part is done now you will submit your article to Ezine Articles. Ezine approval times can vary greatly so it's best if you stay consistent and do submissions every day so you will constantly have traffic going through your affiliate link. If you can afford the premium membership at Ezine, it's well worth it. Have you ever noticed why anytime someone asks about the Premium Membership on Warrior Forum, there's never a lot of answers? Yea you'll get a few, but most of the "better known" members will say it's not worth it. Well, let me tell you it's worth it and a lot more!

Here's what you're not being told. First off, your articles will get approved in about an hour. Now, this may not seem like much, but when you're waiting a week to get an article approved it sucks! No more waiting weeks to get a live article. The best part is that you can schedule the times you want your articles to come out.

Now think about that for a minute. The goal has always been to get your articles put on the "recently published" list at the end of the day. Well now, you don't have to play the game anymore. You can submit your article, and have it timed out for the hour you want it to go live, guaranteeing you to be on that list for the night! Ezine stops approving articles at 6 PM, so just set yours to come out later than 6 PM and you're golden! Your traffic will probably triple what you're used to. More traffic = more sales!

But now look at it from the standpoint of someone who doesn't have a premium account. I know that your articles are only going to come out until 6 PM Eastern time because

that's when Ezine stops approving them. So, if I don't feel like competing with you, I'll load up 10 articles to go live at 7 PM and knock everybody right off the "recently published" list and there is nothing you can do about it. Also, you don't think I'm the only one doing this. Do you? If 20 of us have the premium account and we all do this, you're not going to have a chance of staying on that list overnight which is where all the traffic is to start with. Sad, but that's the way it is. Are you starting to see now why you don't see anyone talking about having the premium account? Because it's a huge advantage! Why am I telling you this? Because I want you to have every possible angle to make money, and that is one big angle.

My recommendation is that you submit 3 articles per day per niche at first if you want to make some decent money. Once you get a few ranking in Google, you don't have to submit that many and can start a new niche. Once you get your first article or set of articles approved, it's time to start backlinking them so you can get them ranked at the top of Google and get free traffic.

Now, because EzineArticles have a PR rank of 6, it's naturally going to rank well right off the bat of being indexed. Many times, it will hold one of the top slots on the front page for your keyword for a day or two after it is indexed. Unfortunately, it's not going to stay there. You are going to have to get some backlinking going on to make it stay.

Now, if you picked your keywords correctly, you would have no problem getting your article ranking well in a short amount of time. The more competition you're up against the longer it will take. But one thing about competition, if you're willing to outwork them you can take their slot. If you do what I'm about to tell you, you will outwork over

95% of the people you are up against.

CHAPTER EIGHT

Backlinking

Let's talk about linking strategies. Now we all know that Google likes it when your links are coming from relevant content. So why don't we just create some relevant content and link them all together. Here's how you do that: There is a great tool called Article Rewriter that can create a few hundred unique versions of your article that you can do these next few steps with. I think it costs like $47.00 but it is worth it as a time saver. You just rewrite each sentence in your article four or five times, and it creates a hundred articles for you that are unique. Many times, you can even get a couple of the rewrites past Ezine's dupe content filters.

Ezine's duplicate content percentage that you can get away with varies between 15% - 20%, so if you have an article that's 80% unique, you can submit that to Ezine as well most of the time. You may very well be able to get three or four articles you can submit to Ezine just by spinning one article.

But look at the amount of work you've saved yourself by spinning. You take 45 minutes to spin an article, and not only do you have enough content to build all these backlinking pages, but you also can get 3-5 new articles you can submit to Ezine Articles. Not bad for 45 minutes! How long would it take you to write 4 new articles? That's not including all the content you would have to come up with for what we are going to do below. Now here's where some will say "you need unique content to do anything decent with, that's just garbage".

WHO CARES if you're not creating unique new content! The only people who are going to care are those who own article directories and those who preach the "you have to write unique and informative articles" crowd, and many times they are doing the exact opposite of what they are telling you. Don't believe everything you read or hear. Bottom line is that article marketing has a lot to do with numbers. The fact is the more content you have out in different places, the more chances you have to make a sale. Do you think the Internet is so small that the same person that read your first article at Ezine is going to then see your Squidoo lens, other articles, Hubpages and anywhere else you post some spun content is going to realize it?

Not likely, but there is a good chance that 1000 different people may see one of them because you have so much content out there. That's why I like Magic Article Writer so much, it's a human spinner that you have to rewrite each sentence yourself. This way all your articles are readable and don't look spun and Google considers them all unique content because their duplicate content percentage is usually under 40% if you rewrite each sentence 5 times.

Now, if you're lazy (like I am now) or you just don't like to rewrite articles, you can go to a human rewriter, and they will do it for you. You can get a test run done. They offer a $5.00 free trial for you to test out their service. They do really good work too. For your article that you are trying to rank, you will need to write another article to point to it. Once you have written this article, you will need to spin each sentence 10 times. I do recommend the second option just because it can be hard to think of 10 different ways to say the same thing, but some people do prefer to do things themselves.

Once you have your article rewritten, it's time to build yourself a giant content funnel. Now, you only need 30% unique content to be considered safe by Google, but the more unique content you have, the better your results are going to be. By rewriting each sentence 10 times, most of your spun versions will be about 80% unique. What you want to do is go to web 2.0 sites such as Weebly or Live journal and start to put 1 spun article on each site. Start with about 4 or 5 of these Web 2.0 sites and put one version of the article on each one of them.

Make sure that within the article somewhere there are two links. One will point to the article you are trying to rank for in anchor text (or your landing page if you're using that instead of an article), and the other link will point to the last page you just created also in anchor text. Make sure that you vary the anchor text a little bit as well. You don't want them all having the exact anchor text as that would be a little unnatural looking. If your keyword is "blue Bats", vary that anchor text to say things like "big blue bats" or "different blue bats" every other page or so. Also, vary the anchor text that you link back to the previous site with as well.

Let's say you start with Weebly, and you post a version of your spun article. Since it's your first page, you're only going to have one link on it for now and that will be your link to the article you are trying to rank. Once you have done that, move on to say Live Journal. You will then place another version of the spun article on Live Journal, but this time you will have two links. One will point to the article you are trying to rank for, the other will point to the Weebly page you just created. Once that is completed, now you can go to another Web 2.0 site such as Scribd. There you will place another version of your spun article and it will also have two links on it: one to the article you are trying to rank for, and one back to the Live Journal page we just created. Do you see what we are doing here? After you have done to where you have four or five sites with a spun version of your article on it all linking back to each other and the landing page, you go back to the first site you created (which in this case would be the Weebly site). Now remember that you only had one link on this page because it was the first one you did, but now you want to go back and put that second link on that page and link it to the last page you just created.

This way you now have a complete circle or funnel that is all pointing to the article you are trying to rank and are also linked together in a circle. Relevant content all linking together and to your article equals loss of link juice! Because the articles we are placing are all around 80% unique, the search engines are going to see this as a great content that is all linking to your article. Now what you do is go out and build another "funnel" just like the one you just did but this time, link to one of the Web 2.0 sites in your original wheel.

Now, this does take time to do, but it also does help you boost your search engine rankings quite dramatically. There is no end to this either. You can build out as much as you want as far as funnels go. Couple this with the other methods I'm about to show you and you'll be kicking ass as far as where your articles are ranking.

Don't forget that you can also blast out these spun versions of articles to the other directories as well. Put one link pointing to the article you want to rank for (or landing page) and another link to one of the Web 2.0 sites you have built. Many times, you'll be surprised that not only will you have your article ranking on the front page, but you'll also get some of these Web 2.0 properties listed up there as well.

Now, again if you're lazy like me, you can automate this whole process with a program called Senuke. Senuke has a free trial for seven days that you can take advantage of. Even if you don't keep it, if you have your content ready to go, those seven days can put you weeks ahead if you use the program. It will automate the link funnel I just described in about 30 minutes. It will also do the things I'm going to list here below as far as pinging, RSS feeds and social bookmarking. It is a weapon.

Now that you've done that, you need to Ping your sites at Pingoat and social bookmark your Web 2.0 sites at Social Marker so you can get even more backlinks. Again, if you're lazy like me, you can use something automated like Senuke (which does bookmarking, RSS submissions and pinging) or Bookmarking Demon Now, each of these sites also have RSS feeds. You will want to submit each of the RSS feeds for your Web 2.0 sites and your Ezine author RSS feed to the RSS sites here. Now you've got some good backlinks going on for your article and it should give you a little boost in Google.

Now this one step, if you do it, willget you above many of the people you will be up against. Put the link funnel together with the rest of the things I'm about to show you and you can dominate almost anything you want.

Another thing to do to get something else to rank and get more sales is to buy another domain name and hosting and install WordPress on it. You can do this easily with Hostgator through your c-panel. What you want to do is buy a domain name around the niche you are targeting. All you are going to do is make a blog and copy and paste every article you write onto this blog. You won't change a thing about the articles you will paste here. You will copy and paste the title and article onto your WordPress blog. The only difference is that you will just put a link to your affiliate sales page at the end of each post. You won't link back to your articles with this, but trust me this will bring you extra money.

If you do this consistently, you will get a good page rank and quick for this blog. Think about it, if you do even two articles a day, at the end of the 30 days you will have 60 posts on your blog. Keep doing it and in three months you'll have 180. You'll have at least a PR of 3 at this point if not higher and probably ranking for various keywords. The last thing you're going to do in this part before I show you how to take over everything you want is to submit a rewritten version of your article to these article directories:

- Go Articles
- Article Dashboard
- Articles Base
- Search Warp
- Buzzle

If you want to push it, you can create videos for each article and those pages above as well as an audio podcast for them. You can submit the videos and podcasts to the social bookmarking sites as well as the RSS feeds for them as well and it will give you even more backlinks.

You can also use a service like Unique Article Wizard and drive thousands of backlinks to your articles. Unique Article Wizard submits different versions of your article to thousands of directories. Link these back to your article and you'll get tons of backlinks. They've got some videos that explain a little bit more of it on their page if you want to look. It's quite a powerful tool! But now I'm going to take you through a few steps further and let you in on a few things that a lot of people won't be doing which will allow you to pass them up. Now I'm sure you've noticed there is a "most viewed" list at the end of each article you see at Ezine Articles. If you're smart about it, it's not that hard to get on that list.

The good thing about being on that list is that not only will you get a ton of views because it gives you instant credibility, but you will also get a backlink from every article that is on your subject. Overnight you can get a few thousand links to your article just by being on that list. In the next section, I'm going to give you a few ways that you can boost not only your views but also how you can get good do-follow links with your keyword in anchor text pointing back to your article.

More Good Stuff

Now that I've shown you a good way to put your backlinking into a category most won't, here's how you can get even more views to your articles and push it up on the "most viewed or 90 days list" if you can get on that list at the bottom of Ezine articles, you are guaranteeing yourself a lot of backlinks and most likely sales!

The first thing you can do is to go into Yahoo! Answers and answer questions about the problem you are trying to solve and leave a link pointing back to your article. If you want to get a little grey hat with it, you can ask a question with one account and answer it with another account. Then give it a day or two and then choose your answer as the best one. This will get a good amount of people to click on your link just to see where the link points. Thus, getting more views to your article and working on getting you moved up onto that "most viewed list" One of my favourite things to do is search in Google for "blogs that use comment Luv".

What this does is show your last blog post when you leave a comment. But instead of leaving a blog post URL, you just put the URL for the article you want to get views for. So now when you leave a comment, if you leave a good enough one, people will click on your link to see your blog post. But instead of a blog post, they will see your article. Hit enough blogs and you can easily get a few hundred views a day like this.

Another thing I like to do is make a stupid video for something and put it on YouTube. When I say stupid, I mean like a guy hitting someone in the nuts with a whiffle ball bat or something along those lines. At the end of the video, you can put a call out that says "to see what he looks like now click here" then you have an arrow pointing to your link which will lead to your article instead. Yea, it's not going to get you any sales most likely, but we're just working on getting your article into the most viewed category.

The reason this is so great is that once it's there, it usually will spend a good 90 days on that list unless someone comes along and knocks you off it. That's 90 days of free traffic and backlinks and remember if you wrote your title as I explained earlier, you'll have no problem getting it looked at. Here's another method using Twitter.com. If you don't have a Twitter account yet, go get one. Go get like 10 of them under different names. Each day you will want to follow as many people as you can or as many as time allows. Many of them will automatically follow you back. After a couple of days, just go back in and delete all the people that didn't return follow you and repeat the process.

Then once you get a few thousand people following you, just send out a tweet that says something like "this pisses me off!" and then leave the link to your article. Of course, you can't do this every day with the same account because people will know not to click on it. That's why you do it with 10 different accounts. Just use the next account a day or so later and so on. This way people won't be able to remember which account it came from last time. You can easily get a few hundred views like this. And if you do it with 10 different accounts, imagine how many views you could get.

All boosting you up onto the "most viewed for 90 days" list. Once you get one article there, just do repeat the processes above on another article. If you stay consistent, you could take over the whole "most viewed for 90 days" list if you use different pen names for the articles.

Don't forget about forums as well. There are usually a good number of forums that will discuss "problems" that we will be solving. Go get in there and join in the conversation. Just put something in your signature that leads back to your article. This way, when someone clicks your signature link, you get another view of your article. There are a ton of ways you can get even more views if you're willing to think outside the box a little bit. These are just a few ways that will make you quite successful if you're willing to put the time in.

Remember, there is no superhighway to success online. If there was, everybody would be doing it. It takes work and dedication, but if you're willing to put in the required effort, success will come. Now let me show you how to scale this stuff up and start putting some serious money in your pocket by outsourcing.

Outsourcing

I almost left this part out on accident, but I got a question the other day about how I got my methods to the point where I can only work about 45 minutes a day and still make 4 figures a month. Here is what I told them, and it is true for everyone reading this as well. The key to everything is budgeting your time the best way you can. Let's say you spend 3 hours a day writing 6 -8 articles. Now let's say that one of those articles gets you a sale for $26.00. You made that $26.00 in 3 hours which works out to a little less than $8.50 per hour.

But what if you took that $26.00 and hired someone to rewrite those 8 articles at 3.00 per hour (which is high, you can get them cheaper) or even $1.50 apiece? At the most, you've just spent $12.00, and you can submit those articles to Ezine if they are 80% unique. You've still got a profit of $14.00 in your pocket and guess what, the 3 hours you would have spent writing another 6-8 articles are now free! You've just created an extra 3 to four hours for yourself and kept a profit of $14.00.

What do you do with your free time? Start writing in another niche! Get a few articles out and repeat the process. Make some money and then pay someone to rewrite them for you and free up more of your time. More profit, more time freed up, less time you must spend! But wait, you still have $14.00 left over from the first 26.00. What you do is outsource someone to do the social bookmarking for you at $2.00 an hour. It will usually take them an hour or an hour and a half to do it. For five days, you can have someone do it all for you, freeing up more time. If you don't want to pay someone to do the bookmarking for you, pick up a bookmarking tool like

Bookmarking Demon or Senuke that does it all.

Make Money

The only question now is what are you going to do with this information? I've given you a way to dominate almost everybody you will come up against when it comes to article marketing. Don't let this be another thing that just takes up space on your hard drive! Take this information and put it to work for you. It will only bring you success! You like money; don't you?

Printed by Libri Plureos GmbH in Hamburg, Germany